D1629641

The Lipizzaners and the Spanish Riding School

Wolfgang Reuter

Pinguin-Verlag, Innsbruck

The publishers are particularly to the photograph archives of Ministry for Agriculture and Foresty for the preparation of the colour photographs.

Copyright 1982 by Pinguin-Verlag
A-6021 Innsbruck
All rights reserved
Lithography: Ifolith, Fotolitho, Innsbruck
Printed by Tyrolia, Innsbruck
Printed in Austria
ISBN 3-7016-2140-3

Contents

The varied history of the Lipizzaner breed

Foundation and development of the stud

In classical antiquity the Karst region by Trieste already had a good reputation for horse breeding. This was particularly true of ancient Aquilea, near where Lipizza lies. The Karst horses distinguished themselves in front of the "quadrigae" in the chariot races of the famous "Circus Maximus" in ancient Rome, and they were also highly prized as war horses.

The Venetians carried on a flourishing horse breeding business at the source of the Timavus – the present day Reka. In the Middle Ages too the Karst stallions enjoyed great popularity with the knightage for tournaments and jousting contests.

These facts may have influenced the Archduke Charles in the year 1580 to found the "Royal and Imperial Court Stud of Lipizza on the Karst" as it was officially titled, on an overgrown estate close to the village of the same name. The wilderness as it then was could hardly be considered a paradise for horses, however, the sparsely growing grass on the chalky ground was particularly nourishing and the air blowing from the Adriatic was full of salt and ozone. All the favourable factors for the rearing of healthy horses were thus present.

In the foundation year Baron Khevenhiller was despatched to Spain to buy breeding stock there for the new stud. He purchased 9 stallions and 24 mares, the ancestors of the Lipizzaners of today. In those days the Spanish horse played a similar role to that played by the English thoroughbred in this century. Originally produced during the Moorish rule by crossing Arab and Berber stallions with the indigenous Iberian breed, it possessed all the advantages valued by the nobility at that time, namely enormous physical strength, combined with light, graceful action and a marked aptitude for dressage.

After the expulsion of the Moors from Spain many European nobles founded studs with Spanish horses. In Italy these won fame with Polesin and Neapolitan strains. Denmark had its Royal stud at Frederiksborg, Germany that of the Princes of Lippe-Bückeburg. Maximilian II of Austria founded the Kladrub Court Stud on the Elbe.

The latter stud specialised more in the production of large-framed carriage horses, but also supplied a top-quality ancestor for Lipizza, the famous Maestoso whose blood flows today in the arteries of descendants of the Maestoso dynasty.

The greatest importance in the breeding of Spanish horses in the Danube Monarchy was without doubt achieved by Lipizza. After the first importation of horses all the conditions for a promising start were at hand. The essential construction work was commenced with a will so that by 1585 the stud farm already had all its buildings and equipment. Six great water tanks had been set up to catch rainwater, thereby circumventing the unfortunate shortage of water. Stables and accommodation were built and enclosed by a wall; a part of the stony ground had been converted into fertile land. Already by 1595 thirty foals could be sent to the ducal stud at Graz. A splendid achievement!

The successor to Charles, Archduke Ferdinand later Emperor Ferdinand II, continued the work at Lipizza with the same enthusiasm as the founder. The emperors Maximilian II and Rudolf II saw to the provision of new bloodstock for the stud. On their behalf, Prosper Colonna purchased new Spanish horses for breeding.

The stud experienced its first period of glory during the reign of the Emperor Leopold I, who, in his role as pomp-loving baroque prince, needed many riding and carriage horses for the court. He took upon himself the task of expanding the Karst stud. His breeding rules issued in 1585 indicate his expert knowledge and even today they can be regarded as exemplary. They proved so beneficial for Lipizza that there was soon a surplus of horses and the provision of fodder from the home estate became a problem. Purchase of Adelsberg and Prestanegg estates removed this difficulty.

In the year 1736 there were 150 brood mares at the stud. At the time of Maria Theresia there were 200. In the 18th and early 19th century, the stallions used as sires were as follows:

Cordova – original Spaniard
Generale
Amico
Lipp, white; imported from the stud of the Princes of
    Lippe-Bückeburg in Germany
Danese; Dane

Superbo

Montedoro

Toscanello

Sultan, white; original Arab

Soliman, brown; original Arab

Dublino

Pluto; original Dane, line founder at Lipizza

Sanspareil, black; Dane

Junker, white; Dane

Conversano; original Neapolitan; line founder at Lipizza

Saltadore, brown; Holstein

Policastro

Morsu, brown; original Arab

Favory, dun; line founder in Lipizza; transferred from Kladrub

Maestoso, white; transferred from Kladrub, line founder

Neapolitano, brown; original Neapolitan, line founder

Allegro, white; original Spaniard

Confitero, black; original Spaniard

Danese, black; original Dane

The above list shows a consistent use of Spanish and Italian stallions, the sires from Denmark and Holstein also being of pure Spanish descent.

The flight from the French

Until 1785 the stud was able to develop undisturbed. But then began a period of misfortune. First came a petition by Herr von Breinl, which seriously proposed dissolving the stud at Lipizza and building up a similar establishment in Galizia. Emperor Joseph II rejected the application. Later, in March 1792, in the face of the advancing French, the complete stud had to be evacuated to Stuhlweissenburg in Hungary. The 300 horses survived the 14-day march without loss. The hardiness of the Karst horses thoroughly proved its worth. In October of the same year the horses returned home. But the French had destroyed the stud building and equipment, as well as the complete stud archives, an irreplaceable loss to posterity.

Rebuilding was commenced at once but on 4th January 1803 an earthquake laid waste the buildings. Scarcely had the stables and farm buildings been put up again when the French threatened the stud for a second time and necessitated the removal of the horses to Diakvar in Slavonia. The spell in exile lasted for six months, then the horses returned and remained in their homeland for two years. Following the Treaty of Vienna in 1809, under which Trieste and Carinthia were ceded to the French, the Lipizzaners once again had to leave their meadows and stables, this time to set out on the long march to Pétska in Hungary.

For six years the refugees remained there in the Theiss plain. The climatic conditions were not favourable for the Karst horses, it began to look as if the breed would lose its identity and die out. Then in 1815 came the order for the return march, and soon the valuable horses were reinstalled in their own, albeit dilapidated home stables. The horses recovered visibly. By systematic pairing and selection, the breed soon regained its earlier level. The transfer of the previously mentioned Maestoso from Kladrub was expecially helpful.

The last century as a Royal Stud

Up to the first world war, Lipizza was spared further serious setbacks. There were still a few Privy Council intrigues regarding the stud, the last of which was dealt with by the Emperor Franz Joseph I. Under his administration the Royal Stud experienced its last period of greatness. The monarch loved the Karst horses and his carriages were drawn exclusively by Lipizzaners.

These "Lipizzanerjucker" as they are known to the experts, were the result of cross-breeding with the Arab stallions Tadmor, Gazlan, Benazet, Samson, Hadudi, Saydan and Siglavy. The reason for this breeding direction was the belief that the Lipizzaners urgently needed fresh blood. And as there were no longer any original Spanish horses to be had in the 19th century, Arabs were chosen. However, a separate dynasty was founded only by Siglavy, who was purchased in 1816. This period was marked by an enthusiasm for experimenting at the stud. The English thoroughbred had just began its triumphant progress through Europe, and had to be tried at Lipizza. The cross-breeding trials did not show the desired success and the progeny were allowed to die out.

In 1870, the stock on the stud farm numbered 5 stallions and 90 mares. The stallions employed were:

1. at any given time one pure Lipizzaner from, in turn, the strains Conversano, Pluto, Favory, Maestoso and Neapolitano
2. Gazlan, full-blooded Arab, purchased in Syria
3. Samson, full-blooded Arab, purchased in the Gaza region
4. Benazet, full-blooded Arab, bred in Galicia
5. Northern Light, English cross-breed

The mares consisted of:

26 Lipizzaner mares of pure Karst stock

26 Arab mares

46 cross-bred mares.

With the above listed stallions and mares, three strains of horses were cultivated: Arabs, Lipizzaners and that from crossing the two. Some of the Arabs were desert horses, others were reared in Europe. The cross-breeds were the descendants of Arab stallions and either pure Lipizzaner or already cross-bred mares. The mating period lasted from December to the end of May. The fertility was very high and the number of barren mares generally stood at less than 10%. The foals were given hay and oats with their dam's milk. They were weaned after five months. From the end of May to the beginning of November the horses were put out to graze, but were given additional hay.

In their fourth year, in early March, the horses went to Vienna, to the Spanish Riding School and to the Imperial Stables for whose exclusive use they were bred. The best brood mares however were picked out beforehand and used for breeding on the stud farm.

In 1915, owing to the events of the war, the breeding stock and the four year old mares were transferred to Laxenburg near Vienna, the male and female yearlings sent to Kladrub. With the fall of the Danube Monarchy, Lipizza was ceded to Italy.

The stock was divided and the raising of Austrian Lipizzaners was continued on the National Stud Farm at Piber near Graz. During the second world war the Lipizzaners were taken to Hostau in Czechoslovakia. There, brood mares and stallions from Piber, Lipizza and Demir Kapija (a Serbian Lipizzaner stud) were united. At the end of the war the position in Hostau became more and more difficult. The irreplaceable breeding stock was threatened with total loss. Then, when the situation seemed desperate, a saviour appeared.

At a performance by the Spanish Riding School which had been put on in his honour in St. Martin in Upper Austria, General Patton met Colonel Podhajski, at that time director of the School, and after a discussion with him decided to go and fetch the Lipizzaner mares back from Hostau. For Patton this advance into as yet unoccupied territory involved considerable risk, for he was not the commander-in-chief and this action far exceeded his authority. Patton gladly put up with the possibility of unpleasant consequences and acted as a horse lover and cavalier. The loss of the herd of brood mares would have meant the end of the Spanish Riding School, for it is dependant on the young horses from the stud for its new blood. Austria and horse-lovers the world over are eternally grateful to General Patton. Hardly had the roaring guns of the second world war been stilled than the Austrian Lipizzaners were able to return to their home at Piber.

The Lipizzaners of today

The Austrian National Stud Farm at Piber can look back on a long tradition of horse breeding. There the Lipizzaners are reared today in the traditional manner of the former Austrian show and parade horse which once laid its special stamp on court ceremonial. Piber has proved an excellent substitute for Lipizza. What was feared after the first world war – a weakened strain and changed characteristics – has not occurred. The horses from Piber are in no way inferior to their cousins born in Lipizza. The six old-established stallion dynasties still exist. They go back to the stallions Pluto, Conversano, Neapolitano, Favory, Maestoso and Siglavy. These horses passed down highly characteristic looks and qualities to their descendants. Thus the representatives of the individual dynasties can readily be distinguished by their outward appearance.

The Plutos, which have Spanish-Danish ancestors, are deep and broad rectangular horses with rather ram-like heads and high set necks. Their movements are vigorous.

The Conversanos have Arab blood. Their appearance is marked by a strong ram-like head, short back, thick hocks and particularly stately gait.

13

The Maestosos are powerful horses with long backs, extremely muscular cruppers and heavy heads. The influence of the Arab blood is apparent from a soft curve of the nose.

The Neapolitanos were able to keep their original characteristics despite the admixture of Arab blood. Tall and more rangy in appearance, they have graceful movements and a high action.

With the Favorys the Arab influence is more noticeable. They are recognisable by their lighter build. However, the soft curve of the nose is more reminiscent of the Kladrub progenitor, a true Spanish horse.

The Siglavys typify the Arab-Lipizzaner. The head is light and noble, the neck more slender than in the representatives of the other lines. The withers are high and the back short. Their action is not so stately as that of their cousins.

Taken as a whole, the Lipizzaners reared at Piber are horses which are remarkable for their noble form, good action, lively temperament, wonderful character and great aptitude for learning in the haute école.

Their girth varies between 61 and 66 ins. Heavy bones, steely tendons and hard, well-formed hooves lend them hardiness and a especial capacity for work. The white colour is predominant in them. This is the result of using Arab stallions to introduce new blood.

In previous centuries there were many blacks, browns, duns, piebalds and skewbalds among the Lipizzaners. This is clearly shown in the painting "Lipizza 1727" by Hamilton.

Nowadays brown Lipizzaners are relatively rare, though

it has become traditional to work with one brown stallion in the Spanish Riding School.

Like all white horses, the foals are born brown, dark brown or mouse grey, and acquire their snow-white coat by degrees between their 7th and 10th year of life. Last of all they lose the dark hairs in their manes and tails.

It is therefore possible to make a rough estimate of a horse's age by its colouring.

The horses have L branded on the lower left jaw and P with the crown on the near hind leg. Besides these, brands wich indicate paternal and maternal descent are put in the saddle area. The stallions have their father's name in the first half of their double name and their mother's in the second half.

Breeding follows the old-established Lipizzaner traditions. Only those stallions are employed as sires which have proved their aptitude for haute école at the Spanish Riding School in Vienna and with it their suitability for fatherhood. The brood stallions are ridden or lunged daily in the riding enclosure provided. The brood mares with foals and the male and female yearlings are housed in large un-partitioned stables. In summer the horses are put out to graze twice a day. During the midday heat they remain in the stables. There they are also watered and given additional oats and hay. The four-year-old mares are generally broken in, and after careful selection by the stud director they are given a place in the famous herd of brood mares. Stallions of the same age go to Vienna and the Spanish Riding School for training.

The rise of the Spanish Riding School in Vienna

Nobody can forget the occasion of his first visit to the Spanish Riding School. Here, in the palace of classical dressage, tradition and precisely handed down riding skills hold sway, and the magnificent building by Fischer von Erlach provides a frame which no other riding school in the world can offer. Before the eyes of the spectator is revealed a world far removed from the bustle of everyday life, and radiating that peace which is essential for work with horses. No word is spoken. Only the dull thud of hooves and creak of leather mixes with the heavy breathing of the stallions. Each performs his duty quietly. In the traditional brown dress-coat, white buckskin breeches, black top-boots and bicorn hat, the riders work their horses without ostentation. All ride in the classical Viennese manner which has produced so many outstanding dressage artists. The leading actors are without doubt the white stallions. They clearly command the scene, and bear witness to the high standard of the haute école in the Spanish Riding School – Vienna.

The Vienna Court Riding School or Hofreitschule can look back on a long history. In 1562 the chroniclers first mention the laying out of a "Roßtummelplatz" – exercise ground for horses – in and around the site of the present day Josephsplatz. According to these records the horses were trained here in the open air, but it was soon realised that riding during the cold winter months was uncomfortable, and also that the schooling of horses in the haute école was difficult without a covered manège. So a provisional wooden building was erected, and in the year 1572 the existence of a "Spanish Riding Hall" was first recorded. This title was given to the establishment as, at that time, only horses of Spanish descent were employed for the haute école, and similarly today only Lipizzaners – the descendants of the famous Spanish steeds – are trained in the Riding School. An imperial command in the year 1681 ordered the construction of a permanent riding school. It was planned to utilise the ground floor beneath the Grand Hall in the Court Library, and to begin riding there in winter 1685. However, the Turkish wars led to repeated delays in the project, until finally it was abandoned. The Spanish Riding School was to be built on a different site, namely there where the "Pleasure Garden of His Majesty the Roman King" is marked on an old town plan of Vienna from the year 1547. Here, between 1729 and 1735 in the reign of Charles VI, the beautiful baroque building housing the Riding School was constructed in the heart of Vienna, between the Michaeler-Platz and the Josephsplatz, by Joseph Emanuel Fischer von Erlach. The original design for the building was sketched by the builder's father. The younger von Erlach was able to inform his imperial overlord of the completion of the Riding School on 14th September 1735. The exterior of the building is not beautiful. It is overpowered by the overdecorated central cupola of the Michaeler façade. In contrast, the Riding School hall is revealed as a magnificent room, full of light, with two galleries and a wonderful, richly ornamented stucco ceiling. Opposite the entrance is the portrait of Emperor Charles VI riding a Lipizzaner stallion. This provides the only patch of colour on the walls of the great white hall.

The manège of the Vienna Hofreitschule was always accounted one of the most attractive in Europe. It became the festive setting for many grand celebrations, riding tournaments and splendid carriage parades. It was here that Maria Theresia staged her grandiose carousel to mark the recapture of Prague. A year later the Riding School was transformed into a ballroom and a grand masked ball was held in honour of the newly-married Archduchess Johanna, a sister of Maria Theresia. After this the manège continued to serve as a worthy setting for balls, carousels and other occasions. Particularly in the controversial days of the Treaty of Vienna, the Winter Riding School provided a meeting place for the crowned heads and the eminent statesmen of Europe. Commerce, too, gained entry to the sanctuary of the School. In the cholera year of 1831 the Vienna stock exchange was transferred to the Riding School. And in 1830 it became the scene of the first public industrial exhibition. Even politics were served by the venerable hall. The first Burghers' Assembly passed their resolutions here in 1848, and shortly afterwards the Austrian Parliament met here. The last carousel was staged in the year 1894. From then on the Winter Riding School was used exclusively for the cultivation of classical equestrian art and the training of the Lipizzaner stallions.

Equestrian art from Xenophon to the present day

The beginnings of classical equestrian art are to be found in antiquity. At that time it was already highly regarded and had reached a considerable degree of development. The oldest surviving equestrian principles were laid down by Xenophon, the cavalry officer, historian and agriculturist. His two books Hipparchikos (the Riding Master) and Perihippikes (Art of Horsemanship) were written in the fourth century B. C. and refer in many places to Simon of Athens, whose writings have been lost. Until the 16th century, they remained the only written works on horsemanship. The riding principles laid down by Xenophon, apart from a few minor technicalities, are still valid today. This is not to say that horsemanship has stood still at the level of that time, but rather it is an acknowledgement of the brilliant conception and accurate judgement of the great Greek general. Many other great horsemen appeared on the scene during the course of the centuries. None was able to invalidate the theories of Xenophon. All could merely try to understand the art of this famous Greek and strive to achieve the aims which he laid down. Xenophon's teachings were intended for the training of war horses. They were the result of careful observation and practical experience. Xenophon required greater cooperation and obedience from the war horse than many a horse, which is entered nowadays for dressage trials, is capable of demonstrating. And in these demands for bending

Courbette à
droite

Courbetten
rechts

Courvetta ad
dextrum

the haunches, raising the body and tractability in the thick of battle are anchored the foundations of the haute école.

Unfortunately, in the years that followed his death Xenophon's teachings were to sink gradually into oblivion.

In ancient Rome, during the confusion accompanying the Migration of Nations, equestrian art was driven ever further into the background; it was also largely supplanted by chariot racing. In the end the Romans had to relearn the management of war horses from the Teutons. But there any similarity with the haute école was non-existent.

During the Middle Ages the art of dressage was but little in demand. The tournament horses had to charge forward in a straight line and, by producing the greatest possible force of impact, help to unseat the opposing contestant.

We first find reawakening of interest in horsemanship with the invention of firearms. Now the cavalry man fighting on horseback needed an agile horse, trained in the arts of the haute école. In fact, many exercises which are shown today in the Spanish Riding School in Vienna date from that period. The obedient stallion rescues its rider with a Capriole from a desperate situation in battle, at the same time repulsing the pursuer with a blow of the hooves. In the Levade he protects his master with his own body from the bullets of the threatening gun. With an elegant Pirouette the mounted pursuer could overtake his fleeing enemy and challenge him to do battle. Thus the horses took an active part in the fighting, and their skill and unswerving obedience decided the victory or defeat of their riders.

The first new impetus toward haute école came from Italy. In 1550 the Neapolitan nobleman Federico Grisone published a new work on horsemanship.

In England it was the Duke of Newcastle who concerned himself with dressage, although the responsibility for having ruined English riders' taste for the haute école must be laid at his door. The cause of this was that the Duke preached the foreshortening of all the movements. As his example he cited Louis XIV's master of the horse who took a quarter of an hour to traverse 150 paces at a gallop.

Twisted necks and distorted action were the consequences of the curb rein which he introduced, and which was an abomination to the English riders who at that time were preoccupied with the newly fashionable horse racing.

In 1588 Georg Engelhardt von Löhneysen published a book on horsemanship and with it drew the attention of German riders to dressage. France made its contribution to equestrian art on the Continent through Pluvinel, Gaspart de Saunier and F. R. de la Guérinière. Pluvinel was promoted to the position of riding master to Louis XIII of France. He had gained his knowledge of the haute école in Naples. In 1632 the master published his life's work:

"Le Manège Royal per Antoine de Pluvinel."

Gaspart de Saunier and F. R. de la Guérinière paved the way for the haute école of the present day.

The first did away with the severe bridlebits of the

22

Neapolitan School and the curb-rein invented by the Duke of Newcastle. The second was responsible for the complete reform of the art of equitation. What he saw to be wrong was replaced by something better. Therein lay his success. First of all he introduced the dressage riding position in place of the "open" position. In the new position the riders' thighs – previously wide apart – were held in close to the horse and used for guidance. De la Guérinière rode all his horses with soft bits. For him relaxation and continuity were of primary importance and prerequisite for the horses' obedience.

The work at the Spanish Riding School

The principles of the haute école as worked out by de la Guérinière became a corner-stone of the training programme at the Spanish Riding School in Vienna. At that time horsemanship there had already reached a high standard. At the opening of the manège, built under Charles VI, 54 stallions from the imperial stud were shown in all the haute école exercises. Responsibility for the training of horse and rider, right up to the present day, has always lain in the hands of the riding-masters or Bereiter and the Oberbereiter.

It is to these men that we are indebted for maintaining dressage horsemanship at its highest level throughout the centuries. They served their apprenticeship at the School and then, as outstanding Masters, passed on their knowledge to the new generation.

Even today great stress is laid on the training of new riding-masters.

The faultless seat which we admire in the riders of the Spanish Riding School is the result of systematic practice on the lunging rein without stirrups. In this way the young riders learn to sit in to their horses without support.

Even the greatest experts at the School often practise on the lunging rein in order to correct at once any fault which may have arisen in their sitting position. The correct seat is imperative for exact guidance of the horse while riding, and also for the general appearance. Horse and rider must look as if they are part of one another. By riding the older, more tractable horses, well versed in the haute école movements, the young rider learns the correct "aids" and a feeling for the exercises of the haute école. Thus the horse becomes the rider's teacher, and this learning from the horse in invaluable. Naturally the experienced stallion notices every mistake and the smallest weakness of the beginner. Consequently the pupil must practise great self-discipline and must keep himself under control when an exercise goes wrong. On no account must he blame the horse for the fault, but rather must he strive to give that precise guidance which the horse once learnt from the experienced Bereiter. For it is the expert instructors at the School who instil their knowledge into the young horses and, through patience and hard work, turn them into well schooled stallions. This training tradition for riders and horses is of great practical value for the Spanish Riding School. The novice rider learns from the horse, and the horse from the trainer. Through this reciprocal education, classical equitation has been cultivated and handed down in Vienna for many centuries.

The purpose and aim of the work at the Spanish Riding School was and is the cultivation of classical equestrian art at its highest level. The training undergone by the Lipizzaner stallions serves this end, at the same time acting as a qualification test used to select the horses for breeding. Thus only the very best stallions, which have demonstrated their aptitude for the haute école, are employed as sires at the stud.

A training plan for the Spanish Riding School was compiled at the end of the last century by Johann Meixner, the Oberbereiter at that time, and the deputy director of the institute, Field Marshall von Holbein. The principles, most of which had previously been handed down by word of mouth, were here brought together and comprise three basic sub-divisions:

1. the forward gaits
2. the lower (or campaign) school
3. the haute école

The first sub-division entails working the horse at the walk, trot and canter on a long line. Keeping the hooves together and shortening the gaits are not yet demanded. The horse's carriage is completely natural.

The lower school is a development of the first stage. The hind legs are bent further under the body, the hooves thus brought closer together enabling the horse to be ridden into all the gaits, figures and turns.

If the maximum degree of haunch bending and body lifting is achieved, and if the horse can perform all the straight forward and complex gaits and raised exercises smoothly and regularly, then he is considered fit to move on to the training level of the haute école. The forward gaits and the campaign school have provided the basic training for this. Every correctly schooled stallion must therefore be a serviceable campaign horse and also be obedient to the rider's touch in the faster movements.

The stallions' training period at the Spanish Riding School begins in their fourth year. First of all they have to get used to their new surroundings.

Caprioles par le
Droite.

Capriol gerad
aus.

Capriolus
rectà.

The happy-go-lucky life on the stud meadows gives way to serious work in the Riding School. At the beginning of their career the young horses are put on the lunging rein for 6 to 12 weeks. In this way they learn to trust their trainer and soon learn the simplest aids and commands. This is of noticeable benefit later on for work in the saddle.

The horses are broken in with great care, for the Lipizzaner matures late, and is not fully grown until the age of 7. For the remainder of the year the young horses are ridden forward with increasing speed and are made more familiar with the rider's aids.

The daily training period is never longer than 45 minutes. The young stallion is ridden with care and consideration, for moderation in the demands made on a horse in his youth allow him to maintain his capacity for work until he reaches a ripe old age. For example the 25 years old stallions at the Spanish Riding School are by no means numbered among the elderly horses. Through years of systematic progress in dressage they are enabled to reach full physical development and can easily cope with the demands made on them. Here it must again be said that the Lipizzaner is a particularly tractable and hardy horse, the result of centuries of carefully planned breeding.

In the second training year there is a gradual increase in the demands made on the stallion. Flexibility is promoted by practising turns and voltes. Sideways movements, full passes and frequent changes of gait and pace increase the degree of control and thus also the concentration. Cadence and timing of the steps improve. The stallion reacts already to the most finely adjusted guidance. During this stage in the training the trot is generally preferred. It gives the rider the greatest opportunity to control the progress of his mount. The swing of the back permits him to sit easily and enables him to measure the degree of relaxation and the correctness of the hindleg action. This work strengthens the muscles, particularly of the hindlegs, and leads to increased suppleness and flexibility. This is the preparation for the canter, which encourages the forward urge but which must never be maintained for too long otherwise the horse tires, no longer springs cleanly, and lands on his forefeet.

Riding through the corners is approached with deliberation and care is taken to ensure that the horse always bends inwards, maintains his rhythm and places the rearhoof exactly in the print of the forehoof. Through this exercise, together with voltes and wide turns bending inwards the horse's body becomes more flexible, his hindlegs are brought into play and a correct angle is achieved. In between times he must be ridden energetically freely forward in a long line, thereby achieving lively steps in the shortened movements. Alternation of the different gaits and frequent changes of tempo increase the alertness, obedience and concentration.

The shoulder-in exercise is practised at a walk, a trot and a canter and serves to achieve the essential flexibility of the shoulders, to improve the action and increase further the general suppleness of the body and the bending of the inside leg. The Traverse, the backward step, and the "cruppers in" are the next exercises and introduce the horse to the double hoof-beat. They increase the turning ability and dexterity.

Basically the training of a School stallion is no different at this stage from that of a dressage horse to be shown at tournaments, except that the exercises are performed with absolute precision. Only on this basis can the demands of the haute école be met.

The Haute école:

The haute école differentiates between exercises on and above the ground.

The movements on the ground are the gallop change, Pirouette, Piaffe and Passage. The movements above the ground are the Pesade, Levade, Mezair, Courbette, Ballotade, Croupade and Capriole. All these exercises are movements drawn largely from nature, cultivated by training and made useful to man. Unnatural movements such as the marching step and certain others are despised by the Spanish Riding School and rejected.

Horses at large perform beautiful Passages or Piaffes when they are excited by an unexpected occurrence. Fighting stallions often execute Courbettes or jump with all four legs off the ground, striking at their rival, thus showing a Capriole. Horses galloping freely change step in mid flight at every change of direction in order to keep their balance. The horses prepared at the lower school acquire perfect balance and precision in their third year. The shortened movements in particular are now worked out while at the same time the stallion's deportment and style are improved. The vigour and liveliness of the steps must not, however, be neglected as a result, but must be brought into play in the sideways movements and the turns. If the horse shows an aptitude for these exercises the haute école training can be commenced. The flying gallop change is prepared by leading the horse into a gallop from both sides. Then the gallop it practised with the change coming in the same place each time, so that the horse can learn the commands. Once it has grasped the regular gallop change it will soon learn to do it after every step. Later the horse must frequently be ridden at a reverse gallop so that he can learn to change from the riders' guidance alone.

In the Pirouette the horse performs a collected canter in a circle. The inner hindleg acts as a pivot for the forelegs and the outer hindleg. In preparation for the Pirouette the Passade is practised and in this figure the hindlegs describe a circle three paces in diameter.

The Piaffe is learnt in hand without a rider. From the shortened trot emerges the cadenced trot on the spot, the Piaffe. A slight forward movement of a few inches is permissible and practical when beginning the Piaffe. Then follows the Piaffe with a rider who however merely sits, quiet and relaxed, to enable the horse to get used to a rider's weight while Piaffing. Guidance is given by the instructor who stands beside the horse, and who later climbs into the saddle himself so that he can actively encourage the horse.

The Piaffe between the pillars precedes the training in hand and with a rider. Work between the pillars, a method introduced by Pluvinel, often gives rise to misconceptions. It requires skill, a sympathetic understanding of the horse and a lot of patience. It is no good putting the horse between the pillars and trying to compel him to piaffe by using a whip. Plenty of praise and very little punishment provide the only way to succeed.

The Passage or Spanish Walk is developed from the Piaffe. In the same rhythm as this high step the horse moves forwards in a measured stride of deliberately suspended motion. With the Piaffe and Passage the haut école training on the ground is completed.

Not every horse is qualified to learn the Pesade, Levade and the jumps. Their talent in this direction is tested between the pillars and then the chosen horses specialise in Levades, Caprioles and Courbettes.

Pesade and Levade from to some extent a link between the ground exercises and those in the air. For both figures the horses are started off with the Piaffe. This developes the hindlegs and their carrying power. In the Pesade the forelegs are lifted to an angle of 45 degrees from the ground. The Levade is the completion of the movement. The horse bends his hindlegs until the hocks are almost touching the ground. The forelegs with bent knee-joints are not lifted so far off the ground as in the Pesade, while the rump is almost parallel with the ground and the whole weight of the body is balanced on the hindlegs. Both exercises can be performed in hand and with a rider.

The Mezair is a succession of Levades. The horse rises into a Levade, touches ground again with the forelegs, brings the hindlegs forward and rises again to a Levade. The forward movement is the main characteristic of the exercise and it can therefore be considered an easier form of the Courbette.

The Courbette is one of the most difficult movements which is performed above the ground. It often takes years before the new generation yields a stallion which has the necessary talent. From the Piaffe the horse rises to a Pesade and, according to his ability, performs two to six forward leaps without touching the ground with his forelegs.

The Croupade is a leap into the air on the spot from a Piaffing position. While the horse is in the air, his forelegs are bent and his hindlegs tucked under his belly.

The Ballotade differs from the Croupade only in the position of the hindlegs. The horse extends these as if to strike and shows his hooves.

The most impressive movement performed above the ground is the Capriole. The stallions indicate their aptitude for this exercise while working between the pillars. The most suitable are those which answer every touch of the whip by striking out immediately with their hooves. The rider first leads the horse into a Piaffe, followed by a Pesade and then into a particularly high Ballotade which becomes a Capriole as the horse kicks out violently with his hindlegs. The whole sequence takes only a few seconds to complete so the Capriole appears as a leap into the air with a simultaneous backward kick. The Capriole is performed between the pillars, in hand and under the rider. It demands the maximum degree of concentration and effort. As in all movements which are performed above the ground, the horse is ridden without stirrups.

Performances

The performances of the Spanish Riding School in Vienna are very popular. They give the visitor an insight into the work of the Institute.

The riding hall with its festive illumination is the scene of a comprehensive programme performed in front of the spectators. At the beginning, the young stallions are presented on the snaffle. Some of them still have the dark coat of youth. They advance with vigour and willingly accept the guidance of their riders. After them, the fully trained stallions make their entry. They are nobly saddled and harnessed. Saddle-cloths embroidered in gold, red and blue show under the grey buckskin saddles, and the gala bridles shine in the spotlight. The riders pay homage to Emperor Charles VI, the Creator of the Winter Riding School. With an incomparable elegance they begin their work with all paces and figures of the haute école. The horses are light on the reins – guided almost invisibly, they perform Pirouettes, Traverses and gallop changes with a unique easiness and lightness. They are followed by horses performing their exercises in hand. We now see Piaffes along the wall and between the pillars, and school jumps without a rider. "Pas de Deux" and "Pas de Trois" are presented by fully obedient schooled stallions showing all the figures and exercises with great exactness.

A speciality presented by the Spanish Riding School is their work on the long rein. The instructors walk beside the hindlegs of the stallion and show all the difficult figures which have already been performed with a rider in the saddle. The horse reacts merely to rein guidance.

This work requires fully trained stallions obedient to the slightest touch.

The figures "above ground" are a special attraction for the onlookers. Powerful stallions jump their Caprioles, whereas others rise in Courbettes or stiffen in a Levade. The great School Quadrille with eight or twelve horses is the traditional finale of the performance. It reminds us of the carousels of old times. A unique picture – the white horses all executing the same figures and supple movements in complete harmony with their riders.

Postscript

The Lipizzaners and the Spanish Riding School have withstood many hardships over the centuries. It was not always easy to protect the horses and institutions from thoughtless acts. Especially after the two World Wars, the continued existence of horses and Riding School was seriously endangered. Yet there have always been men whose courage and personal sacrifices have preserved these wonderful horses and the classical haute école for the delight of future generations.

Performances in many European countries and in America have given the Lipizzaners and the Spanish Riding School the opportunity to make friends all over the world. For Austria they are the remnants of a precious cultural tradition and representatives of an art whose support and development is a noble duty in our days of haste and restlessness.

Stutenherde mit Fohlen auf der Weide
Group of mares and foals in the field

Seiten 38/39: Heimkehr von der Weide
Pages 38/39: Return from the field

Seiten 40/41: Mutterstuten in Lipizza im Jahre 1727,
Gemälde von G. Hamilton
Pages 40/41: Brood mares at Lipizza in 1727, painting
by G. Hamilton

Lipizzanerstuten im Gespann
Lipizzaner mares in harness

Seite 43: Vorführung im Schloß Hellbrunn, Salzburg
Page 43: Performance in Hellbrunn castle, Salzburg

Lipizzanerhengst im Staatsgestüt Piber
Lipizzaner stallion at the National Stud, Piber

Seite 44: Passage, auch Spanischer Tritt genannt, unter
Oberst H. Handler
Page 44: The Passage, also called the Spanish Walk,
demonstrated by Colonel H. Handler

Dieser Lipizzanerhengst kann Araberblut nicht ver-
leugnen
This Lipizzaner stallion cannot deny his Arab blood

Seite 47: Am langen Zügel
Page 47: On the long rein

Gehorsam am Zügel
Obedient to the rein

Seiten 48/49: Kapriole, Gemälde von G. Hamilton
Pages 48/49: Kapriole, painting by G. Hamilton

Seite 51: Courbette an der Hand
Page 51: Courbette in the hand

Der einzige Braune: Levade an der Hand
The only brown: Levade in the hand

Seite 52: Oberst H. Handler bei einer Vorführung in
der Reithalle
Page 52: Colonel H. Handler at a performance in the
Riding Hall

Pessade
Pessade

Seite 54: Levade unter dem Reiter
Seite 54: Levade with rider

Seiten 56/57: Einreiten zur großen Schulquadrille
Pages 56/57: Preparing to do the Grand Quadrille

Kapriole an der Hand
Capriole in the hand

Seite 58: Kaiser Karl VI. Zeitgenössisches Ölgemälde
an der Stirnseite der Reithalle
Page 58: Emperor Charles VI, contemporary oil painting opposite the entrance to the Riding Hall

Pas de Trois
Pas de Trois

Seite 61: Pas de Deux
Page 61: Pas de Deux

Die große Schulquadrille

The Grand Quadrille

Seite 62: Einreiten zur Schulquadrille
Page 62: Preparing to do the Quadrille

Seiten 64/65: Der Leiter der Spanischen Reitschule,
Brigadier K. Albrecht, und seine Mitarbeiter

Pages 64/65: The director of the Spanish Riding School,
Brigadegeneral K. Albrecht, and his staffs

Pirouette rechts, Gemälde von G. Hamilton
Pirouette right, painting by G. Hamilton